BE THE

YOU WISH YOU HAD

40 Power Lessons To Become A Powerful Dad

CLAIM YOUR FREE
EXTRA RESOURCES

BLOG
VIDEOS
PODCAST
YOUTUBE
ETC.

Go To:

BeTheDadYouWishYouHad.com/Extra

BE PRESENT
BE A NEW STATISTIC
BE THE DAD YOU WISH YOU HAD

WHAT READERS ARE SAYING

Unofficial guide to great parenting!

Forty insights to creating a respectful relationship with your child - the must have guide for all Dads, Moms and even uncle Chris.
Simple tools for success - face to face communication, positive reinforcement and engagement while learning to not use the word "NO".
My favorite - was lesson 15 - poignant description of how musical experiences create life long memories.
Execution of the process in its totality quickly becomes a routine for successful dynamic relationship with your kids.

- Chris Jardin
(Uncle to two boys)

I wish I had this book when my kids were young...

Ryan's book "Be The Dad You Wish You Had" is the perfect addition to a new dad's new life. The best time to start being the best dad possible is today, and with Ryan's lifelong lessons, you can start now. I wish I had learned these lessons when my children were younger. I did okay, I love my children and they love me... but I could have been more present and proactive had I known just a few of the 40 lessons he shares. Do yourself and, more importantly, do your kids a favor and not only buy this book... but read it and use the wisdom Ryan shares with you!

- Charles Woolsey
(Father of two adult children)

Amazing resource for Dads!!

WoW! This is such a great resource. I wish I would have had this when we had our first. I love the way he explains things in a simple, easy to implement way. Finally, a book for dads with the How's and the Why's. I could not put this down! I will definitely be keeping this close by!

-Greg Harvey
(Father of three)

If you are a man that has doubts...

If you are a man that has doubts of how to parent, this is definitely the book for you. No matter what sex you are, this is a must read, so that you can totally see what it's like to raise a child from a true man's perspective. I must say once again, totally blown away because I have a lot to learn from this.....

- Paul Ybarra
(Father of 3)

I agree that not all first time or bonus Dads have had great role models

From the book title, you may scroll by because you think "it's just for Dads" it's not. I agree that not all first time or bonus Dads have had great role models. With that said this book is for any first-time parent, a bonus parent, grandparent, or even a parent that has children and wants to communicate and make sure they are doing the best they can this book is fantastic. We have a tendency to over think things with our kids or talk and don't really listen. Ryan Roy has written the book in such a way that it breaks it down and makes you think, "that is something simple, I can do that".......but also reminds us, parenting isn't one problem and done gig.
I love how it is written as a tool. Not a book you can just read through and put up on the shelf, it is an action book, a when you come across this issue of parenting grab the book and look for suggestions.
I have worked and volunteered for years in shelters, dealing with parents, new foster parents that would benefit from these 40 tips. The title may grab you but don't be fooled it's not just for Dads and I highly recommend it for anyone wanting to better understand how to be the best influence for the children in their lives.

- Lisa Bechtol
(Mother of two and Grandmother of four)

Absolutely Awesome Book! Excellent Tips!

This is an absolutely awesome book! With the lessons in this book, you are going to want to use them right now with your children. This is a book that will not gather dust on a bookshelf. I see this as a regular resource for dads to read time and time again. Excellent, powerful tips for dads to make a huge, positive impact with their children.

**– Cynthia Bazin
(Lasar Focused Mentor and mother of two)**

This is an amazing book for all dads

This is an amazing book for all dads, however, I feel this should be read by BOTH parents. This book has so many great principles in it for any new or existing parents. All the lessons will have you thinking and really reconsider how you parent your child. One that comes to mind is saying NO and I will leave it at that. Definitely get this book and read it and absorb as much of the information as possible. Then READ IT AGAIN!

**- George Pitts
(Father of a one-year-old)**

Perfect blueprint to be a GREAT dad!

This book is a perfect resource for all dads and dads-to-be. The principles covered in this book are clear, concise, and easy to understand. Being a brand-new father is a scary feeling, but this book will prepare you to be GREAT. Even if you already have a two-year-old (like me) there are many lessons to learn and this book is a huge help. Do yourself and your children a favor and buy this book, but more importantly - put into practice. Thank you for putting this into the world.

**- John Skistimas
(Father of a two-year-old)**

Powerful Lessons for Any Dad (or Parent for that matter)! A Must Read!

To any parent, would-be-father or current dad, this is an invaluable resource. My wife and I plan on having kids in the future and this book of lessons will definitely be part of our parenting resources. Being the best father that we can be I believe is something that all dads desire. Why not arm yourselves with the tools to do so. A lot of the lessons really resonated with me (and had me thinking back to my own childhood - both positive and not so positive experiences). And it gave a lot of clarity to why a lot of things happened the way they did. And it helped reinforce why I want to do all I can to be the best father I can be.

I encourage you to read this book, learn this book, invest in you and your child's relationship and help become the father you want to be and your child/children deserve.

**- Rodney Smith
(Uncle of one)**

Great basics in this book!

I enjoyed reading Ryan's book. Children grow fast, and if you follow Ryan's advice you won't miss their childhood when you are needed the most.

Presence, communication and respect are the foundational principles in this book. Ryan writes in practical terms about these principles and what they look like in action. Easy to read with basic examples for each topic. If you are a new dad, a soon-to-be dad or a dad working on doing better, this book will bring some great basics into focus for you. Being a parent is no easy feat. This book can help!

**- Anne DiDomenico
(Mother and Grandmother)**

Great book! Ryan makes it easy to understand how to put these important principles into practice!

Great book!! You can have all the "knowledge" in the world, but it is useless if you don't understand how to put it into practice. Ryan does a great job of connecting important principles to real life scenarios. He makes it easy to understand how to put the principles into practice!

**– Geoff Libby
(Uncle of four)**

Awesome and a must read...

This book is awesome and a must read for any new Father. Ryan has excellent insight and experience to share. It also shows that if you are willing to be conscious you can give more than you received. Do you dare to participate in your child's life? It may be the most rewarding thing you ever do.

**– James Brooks
(Father of three)**

Now There Really is an Instruction Manual

Growing up as an orphan, I clearly see all of the things that were missing from my upbringing. My foster father was kind and loving, but did not have this kind of a roadmap for me or my five foster siblings. Ryan took the time to learn, out of desire to release his own pain, and be the best father he could, to find the tools to make sure he could give himself the best chance possible. There are no letters behind my friend's name. He has however created an easy to access, understand, and use set of tools that any man can apply to nurture his family! Like much of life these are simple and not necessarily easy to do. But having watched him over the four years I have known him, the results speak for themselves! Read this book for your children and for your wife. It's the best gift you can give them and yourself.

–Russell Dennis

What a simple and profound read!

There are so many parenting books out there and what I love about Ryan Roy's 'Be the Dad You Wish You Had' is that it's a simple, actionable, distillation of the fundamentals that will enable any parent to set themselves and their kids up for success. A great read for new parents and refresher for those looking to be more mindful parents.

–Stephanie Bryant
(Mother of two)

The journey Ryan took me on through his 40 very common sense rules brought me tremendous joy. He truly subconsciously demonstrates that Parenting truly is ...

I am a proud father of a flourishing teen girl. The journey Ryan took me on through his 40 very common sense rules brought me tremendous joy. He truly subconsciously demonstrates that Parenting truly is a verb. Mentally making declarative statements backed by action are truly the tools in which we can use to define the attributes of nurturing. Exploration, reasoning, experimenting and yes the ability to get hurt are all beneficial to our own learning and provide the evidence that our children will benefit as well. It would be really awesome, if parents would take the short amount of time to digest Ryan's message, and go be creative. Turn the Fridge into daily reminders for the parents and the child on how we can not only be better dad's, but a united team as parents.

-Ryan Miller
(Father of one)

Must Read for Every Dad

This book is a must read for every dad. All of the lessons in this book are so simple, but simple does not mean it's always easy to do. Ryan lays out 40 simple ways of becoming your child's hero. It's up to you to apply these simple lessons if that is what you want. Every man had a childhood hero. When your child thinks of who their hero is as an adult, wouldn't you want to think "DAD"!?

-David McCormack

Easy to read instructional manual

This book is an easy to read, instructional manual to change the trajectory of how we can empower our children to become confident and well-rounded adults, with instead of NO NO , a YES YES. Catch them doing something right and allowing them to think and find the right answer on their own. This book helps parents to create an environment which allows them to soak up knowledge during the most formative years of their life and to teach parents to spend quality time with their children.

-Nancy Berg

This should be in your top three go-to parenting books!

First, let me start by saying this book is not just for men! It should be read by any parent or person that is in any way, shape, or form, caring for children of all ages. As a young man, I married into a ready-made family with three young boys. I certainly did not have the tools with which to raise my stepsons. I had not grown up with any type of male influence in my life so I was quite literally raising them by the seat of my pants via everything I learned in the "real world university." I truly wish I had been able to read these 40 tips back then. Now, as a 49-year-old, I am blessed to be a grandfather to 5 wonderful grand kids and the step dad to two more great adult kids. Because it is never too late to learn how to communicate, I look forward to using the newfound knowledge and wisdom from Ryan's book to help nurture, raise and empower them. Ryan has an exceptional talent of putting these tools into terms that are not only easy to understand, but simple to incorporate into daily living. I assure you that after reading this book you will be just as pleased as I am.

-David Rice
(Father of three, grandfather of five)

Must Read for New or Experienced Fathers

For those of us that didn't have a great father role model in our lives, and we want better for our kids than we got, this book is a must read. Although I wish I had this book before I had My first son, it's never too late to become a better dad.

–Mark Starr
(Father of four)

A life-changing read! For your child AND for you!

I have to agree with the review that stated "I wish I had this book when my kids were younger!" As a mother of 3 teen daughters, I saw so many practical lessons I could've applied to make a positive difference in their lives AND mine! Applying the simple and practical lessons in this book will absolutely create bonds that will last a lifetime, and empower you to raise a confident, joyful, successful child. Not only that, it will help you as a father (and mothers... you too!!) be fully present to fully ENJOY each stage of parenting! Not only do I recommend this book to any parent at any stage... but what an incredible GIFT IDEA for new or expecting parents! It will encourage discussion between mom and dad that will create a unified strategy to set your family up for a lifetime of happiness! Also - for you exhausted new parents - the lessons are quick and easy to read!

-Debi Bellville
(Mother of three)

The truth is a dad plays a major role in a child's life...

Truth is a hard thing to sell because it isn't pretty, it hurts, and it also makes us work; it is also beautiful because it provides knowledge and growth.

The truth is a dad plays a major role in a child's life and we do the best we can and hope the outcome looks like a stable to successful adult when we are done.

The truth about this book is that it is the truth about the work it takes to be a great dad, but because the author simplifies the lessons, the reality of being a great dad seems like less work and more just being present. The author made me feel that being a great dad is attainable and whether intentional or not, he also did a great job reinforcing ideas that would make one not be just a great dad, but a spouse, or a child. The lessons transcend fatherhood and delve into the world of strong relationships.

The title would suggest this book is for men that didn't have a great dad; it is, but it is also for all parents who wonder what it is going to take to nurture a child and continuously have a meaningful relationship with them.

–Dorian Santiago

HOW TO USE THIS BOOK

I hope you enjoy reading *Be The Dad You Wish You Had*, as much as I enjoyed writing it.

For the first 5 years of my son's life, I continually read parenting books, magazines, blogs and internet posts on "how to parent". I read them because I wanted to know how to be a good parent. More important than knowing how to be a good parent, is doing the action necessary to be a good parent.

As you read through the lessons in this book you may start to think, "this is some really basic stuff". I would not argue that. What I would encourage each of you to do is these basic/simple things. Over time, with consistency, doing the little things will eventually lead to success on your parenting journey.

I've often said that "life is simple, people complicate it". These 40 lessons are so basic and simple, but if not implemented you will never know if they will work.

I'll also say that many things that are simple, are not always easy to do. We all know of simple concepts that lead to success that are not easily implemented.

Save 10% of our income and invest it at 8% return for 40 years and retire a millionaire. Simple, but not easy to do.

Eat Healthy and Exercise and you will lead a healthy lifestyle. Yet over 66% of the US population is overweight or obese. Simple, but not easy to do.

Follow the 40 lessons in this book and have a healthy happy relationship with your children for a lifetime.
Simple, but not easy to do.

I encourage you to reference this book several times throughout your parenting journey. When the time is right to create a Family Tradition, (Lesson 34) do so.

When its time to do Skin to Skin (Lesson 2), do so. Make sure you take that opportunity; you only get those opportunities early in the parenting process. You may feel "weird", but it is only because you have never done it before.

Everything in this book is here for a reason. It has worked for my family and me.   I felt a strong conviction to share it with you, the reader.

I encourage you to.....

BE THE

YOU WISH YOU HAD

ABOUT THE AUTHOR

Ryan Roy's father abandoned him at the age of five. Not having a father figure in his life, parenthood stirred a tremendous amount of doubt and fear in his ability to be a good father himself. Ryan decided to gather as much information as he possibly could to be a "good father." Reading parenting books, magazines, articles on the Internet, soliciting advice from friends, listening to doctors and even heeding the advice from some perfect strangers.   He then implemented those ideas with his own family and put together these 40 parenting strategies for you the Reader.

He is an avid sports fan, enjoys cooking, enjoys travel and his most important and favorite thing to do is to be the father to his two boys.

Empowering fathers to be an active part in their child's life is his passion.

Ryan's Mission is: To Have the Respect of His Adult Children. No Thing or No Fling should ever get in the way of that.

What does that mean? It means to think before you act. Work, Money, Car, House (No Thing) should ever come before my relationship with my children. No Fling (moment of weakness) should ever come between the trust of his wife or child. All of your actions have consequences. The last thing a father would want for his son or daughter is for them to lose respect for him because a moment of weakness.   I believe it is the desire of all parents to eventually have the respect of their adult children.

INTRODUCTION

I want you to know that I am not a child psychologist. I want you to know that I do not have a degree in childhood education. I want you to know that I am a regular guy who has a burning desire to be the best father I can possibly be.

These ideas are not unique to me and I did not dream these lessons up. These happen to be a collection of advice given, advice sought after, and knowledge gained through a tremendous amount of parenting books, magazines and internet articles consumed over the first five years of my child's life.

These are only some of the things I have done; and how I believe they have positively affected my son. These strategies work only if you implement them. People want guarantees. I guarantee if you do not implement the lessons in this book, you will NOT get the results you desire.

It takes a great deal of time, dedication, and discipline to be a great dad. It takes a great deal of time, dedication, and discipline to be successful at anything.

The mere fact that you are reading this book, let's me know you have what it takes to be a tremendous parent. My wish is for you to implement these things slowly and consistently over time.

This entire book is based on three basic principles.

1. Spending time with your children
2. Communicating well with your children
3. Giving respect and getting respect

You may be thinking, *why do you assume I don't spend time with my children?* The question is not: are you spending time with your children? It's not that you aren't showing up. The question is: how are you showing up? There is a difference between *time* and *quality time*.

You may be thinking: *I communicate with my children*. Screaming, yelling, and talking down to them is not effective communication. That may be the behavior that you were brought up with in your home. It may be what you were accustomed to, but it certainly is not considered "effective or communication." You may look to your own childhood and say, "I did not like being talked to that way." Programming dictates the same behavior if you are not conscious enough not to change it. By programming I mean, this is what you were taught through your parents' actions, therefore this is the behavior you automatically default to using.

You may be thinking; *my child needs to respect me no matter what*. However, the reality is respect is earned. Creating boundaries is a great way to earn respect.

You may notice that if you follow the first two principles, spending time and communicating, respect will naturally be earned.

BE THE DAD YOU WISH YOU HAD

DEDICATION

This book is dedicated to Eddie Roy, the man on my birth certificate, who physically took care of me for the first five years of my life and financially supported me until I was eighteen. At twenty-five years old, I discovered he is not my biological father. Nonetheless he offered open doors to me. He raised three amazing children of his own, adopted two other amazing children and all of them are better people for having him as a father. I am blessed to be loved by this man. Thank you for inspiring me to complete this book.

This book is a living document of the important things I feel have been critical in my son's first five years of life. I am extremely blessed to have imparted these lessons into his life. I am blessed to have discovered the lessons I'm going to share with you. I am blessed to have had the patience to implement them. I also am blessed to be able to share many of the things I feel it takes to be a successful parent, and more specifically, a father.

BE THE
DAD
YOU WISH YOU HAD

SPECIAL THANKS TO:

My wife Lisa. Without her love and support, this book would not even be a possibility.

Laura Royer for encouraging me to share my parenting strategies.

Dorian Santiago for assisting me in conveying my thoughts on paper (editing).

Charles Woolsey for helping me with the publishing of this book.

Table of Contents

FATHERHOOD STATISTICS

STATISTIC #1

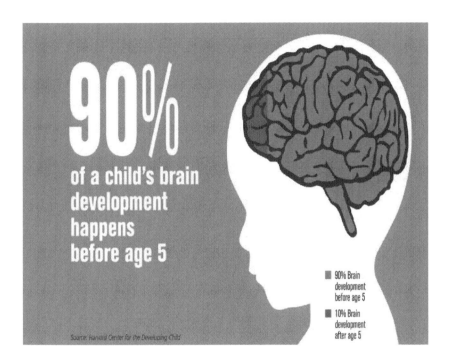

Do You Want to Be a Statistic?
OR
BE THE DAD YOU WISH YOU HAD

FATHERHOOD STATISTICS

STATISTIC #2

The average father in the US looks his children in the eyes less than 15 minutes per week.

Do You Want to Be a Statistic?
OR
BE THE DAD YOU WISH YOU HAD

FATHERHOOD STATISTICS

STATISTIC #3

The average working family spends 7 minutes of dedicated time a day with their children.

BE THE DAD YOU WISH YOU HAD

Do You Want to Be a Statistic?
OR
BE THE DAD YOU WISH YOU HAD

FATHERHOOD STATISTICS

STATISTIC #4

80% of all the hours you will ever have with your children will be in their first 18 years. Therefore, 28% of that time will be before age 5. Make it count. Repetition is the key to learning for all of us, especially young children.

Total Hours Spent With Your Child

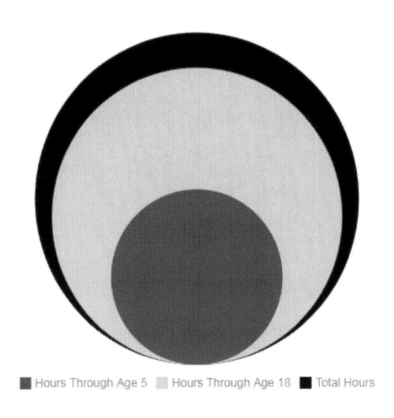

■ Hours Through Age 5 ▨ Hours Through Age 18 ■ Total Hours

Lesson 1
Educate Yourself

Educate Yourself.

Read as much as you can about being a parent before your first child is born (magazines, books, articles, etc). Once the baby is here, the focus becomes the child. Sleeping and adapting to having 24-hour care for another human being is the focus, not the "how to". The first 6 months are a blur. Preparation is key to becoming a successful parent.

Preparation is the key to success for anything. The more parenting magazines, books, and websites you can read the better prepared you will be for anything that may come your way.

Take classes, talk to your doctors and seek advice from trusted parents in your circle.

I remember thinking to myself, *"Why do I have to go to a breast-feeding class?"* But when I got there, I learned so much about what my wife would go through. I was then able to comfort her when those challenges arose. I look back and am grateful for being open-minded enough to attend all the courses, but most specifically the breastfeeding class.

Another course we took was child care 101. We learned how to change a diaper. You may be thinking, *"how difficult could it be to change a diaper?"*It's not easy when the most precious thing in the world to you seems so fragile and you don't want to break it. I'm grateful I took that class.

I remember reading *The Expectant Father* and learning about what my wife was going through during her pregnancy. That book gave me the patience and knowledge to be able to comfort and understand that her hormones and emotions were all over the place. Understanding those issues gave me the patience to get through some of the more difficult days. I knew it was not personal; it was a part of being pregnant. She was not taking things out on me; she was reacting to the change in her body, and I happened to be the closest person on whom to vent.

I remember using Facebook as a resource. I private messaged all of my friends from high school who had already had children and asked them for the one piece of advice they wish somebody had given them. I received some incredible answers and wisdom.

All I am saying is do not wait until you are six feet deep into the pool of parenting to learn how to swim. Start at the steps of conception and get used to it while you are still awaiting your tiny miracle. I hope you are reading this book before you are a father, so you can be more successful at being a parent. If not, it's never too late and the nuggets in this book will get you prepared for the entire journey of parenthood.

Lesson 2
Skin to Skin

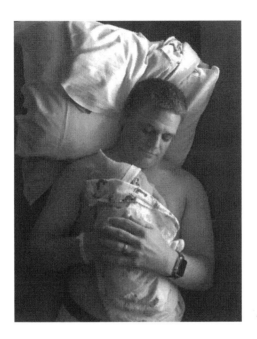

Skin to Skin.

Connect immediately – Skin to Skin – let your child hear your heartbeat to know it is a place of comfort within a few hours after being born, or as soon as possible.

We learned in one of the classes that it is important for a child to have skin to skin contact with mom. The first night in the hospital, my son was having challenges sleeping. My wife was frustrated because he hadn't quite latched on to breast-feeding. They were both tired and frustrated. I took off my shirt, I laid him on my chest, and he fell asleep for the first time on his own. He heard his father's heartbeat and connected. He not only knew his mother's heartbeat was a safe place, he now knew his father's heartbeat was a safe place also. Connect with your child immediately.

Mom had the opportunity to connect physically for nine months. This is your opportunity to connect physically for the first time. It allows the child to bond with you and you with him or her.

Lesson 3
Change Diapers

Change Diapers.

A perfect stranger gave this gem of advice and it made perfect sense to me. Bonding and connecting to your child is such an intimate experience. A great deal of trust is developed between you and your little one. Take every opportunity to gain that trust.

This is something many dads feel is the mother's job. There is no "mothers" job to do. There is no "fathers" job to do. This is an opinion based on my experience. When you change your child's diapers they learn to trust you. They know you'll do anything for them. But if you choose to do certain things and not others, your child will learn you can be relied on for certain things. Why? Because you've shown the child you will only do certain things. This is what's called conditional love. Unconditionally love your child by changing their wet or soiled diapers. Having a soiled or wet diaper is not comfortable for them. Your job is to comfort your child no matter what. That is your duty as their parent.

Lesson 4
No Baby Talk

No Baby Talk.

Talk to your child as if you are having a conversation with anyone else. You do not know when they are going to understand what you are saying. You cannot put a timetable on that. If you talk to them with dialects such as baby talk (Goo Goo, Ga Ga), they will in turn learn to speak that way. Children learn from us and mimic what we do and say. If you speak to them in baby talk, or don't speak to them often, it should be no surprise if they have a difficult time learning to speak for themselves. You are only hindering their speech progress. This is no laughing matter.

When I say talk as if you are having a conversation with anyone else, I mean in the tone and words you use. Children may not understand larger words, but at one point they did not understand small simple ones. Why not engage them in the everyday terminology an adult uses so when those words are introduced to them, and when they are ready to, they understand them. You will know when they are ready. They will ask, "Dad what does _____ mean?" Or they will figure it out through contextual clues.

The possible result of speaking baby talk (Goo Goo, Ga Ga), is they may develop a speech impediment. They only mimic what they are taught. If they are taught to speak any certain dialect or tone, that is what they will mimic, especially if they are only around mom or dad who is speaking to them in those tones. Single parents out there, be especially aware so you do not hinder their growth in areas of annunciation, vocabulary, and comprehension.

Lesson 5
Talk at Eye Level

Talk at Eye Level.

When you speak to your child, take the opportunity as often as possible to get down to their level and look them in the eyes. If you look down at them, it's a position of superiority and it can be intimidating to a child. Whenever you can, become more physically equal so they will be comforted. Talk to them like adults, smile and laugh as much as you can, but always look them in the eyes. In return they will respect you and they will develop the habit of looking at you when you speak. This is foundational for a strong relationship of long term mutual respect.

Take the opportunity to do this while feeding your child, on the floor during tummy time, while having an encouraging discussion, during a teaching moment and most importantly, whenever they do something you may not approve of.

Get down to their level and talk to them in calm tones. They understand more than we give them credit for.

Lesson 6
Tummy Time

Tummy Time - Challenge them from the start.

Always challenge children. Do not limit them or put your own self-limiting beliefs on them. Try to be very conscious of this. When my son was seven days old, I put him on his tummy for the first time. He struggled to lift his head. He struggled to lift his arms. He was frustrated, but it was a moment of growth. I was there the entire way. As I recorded the event with my cell phone, I said to him, "The faster you can get up the faster you can move out be a productive member of society." That may seem harsh and insensitive, however, it's the truth. The more you empower your children to do things, the faster your children will grow and the better off they will be.

Tummy time, early and often, will grow their physical strength and set them up for future challenges and growth they will face in these formative years. This is not only one of their first lessons as a child, but one of your first lessons as a parent. Can you push them beyond what you think they are capable of?

Lesson 7
Anticipate Their Needs

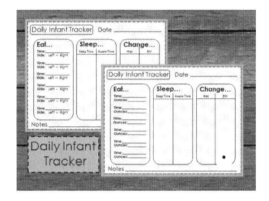

Anticipate Their Needs.

The needs of a newborn are fairly simple. There are essentially three times a baby cries:

1. When they are hungry
2. When they are, wet or soiled
3. When they are in need of attention/comforting

When you are able to create a schedule that adheres to their needs, your child will cry less often.

Track when you feed your child, when you change your child, and when your child goes to sleep and for how long. After the first six weeks, they will start to develop a routine. If you are consistently addressing the NEEDS before they become a concern for your baby or child, your child will not have to speak in the form of crying as often.

Lesson 8
Create a Schedule

Daily Activity Schedule	
9:00 AM	Organized Free Play
10:00 AM	*Morning Snack*
10:30 AM	Arts & Crafts
11:45 AM	Story Time
12:00 NOON	Lunch
1:00 PM	Nap Time, Quiet Time (w/ movies), *or* Table Play Activities
3:00 PM	Story Time/Music
3:30 PM	*Afternoon Snack*
4:00 PM	Game Time
5:00 PM	Clean Up

The above schedule is subject to change without prior notification.

Create a Schedule – humans crave schedules, structure and predictability.

Create a schedule for your child so they know exactly what is going on and stick to it. My wife and I bought a book called *12 Hours and Twelve Weeks*. The book promised to have your newborn sleep 12 hours through the night by the twelfth week. That is a Godsend to new parents as we lack sleep and rest. The sooner you create that schedule for your child, the sooner you get a sense of normalcy.

As children grow older their schedules shift ever so slightly. Adapt and grow in the direction you want to go. Remember you are the parent. If you do not train your child, your child will train you. Which do you prefer?
You may think your life is hectic. Your life can be hectic but the child's life does not have to be hectic. Get them on a consistent schedule of predictability.

First thing in the morning, immediately change their diaper. It lets them know you are taking care of that need.

One of my favorite things to do when my son was an infant was to make his bottles with him. I would put the water with the formula and I would do it all with him in my arms. I would tell him what I was doing every step of the way. Then I would put the cap on the bottle and I would say to him, "Now we have to shaky, shaky, shaky" (shaking the bottle to mix the water and formula).He laughed hysterically and always made his bottles with me.

He always had nap times on the hour, for about an hour (9:00-10:00am and 1:00-2:00pm for the first year).

Feeding times were the same 6:00am, 10:00am, 2:00pm and 6:00pm

Changing times were essentially the same. If he was wet or soiled, it was changed as soon as discovered.

I would ask you to be the parent who understands diapers are not ultra-absorbent. Children do feel it... if not the moisture, the weight of their excretion. Not immediately changing diapers is understandable in circumstances such as trips in the car for a couple of hours. Do not be lazy when it comes to the comfort of your child. By being lazy, you make them uncomfortable and in turn they will make your day uncomfortable too. It is not worth it.

Yes, we went through 10 diapers per day. He never had to cry for food, a dirty diaper, or attention, because he always received all three. Dads, help create a routine for mom and stick to it.

Lesson 9
Itsy Bitsy Spider

Itsy Bitsy Spider, Patty Cakes, Head-Shoulders-Knees and Toes.

These are all simple games that you can play with your child. They are fun and interactive. They typically have some type of rhyme, and they allow you to look at your child at eye level, which helps you connect. There is usually a ton of laughter which is another connector. I suggest you play these games as often as possible. I just played one of these games with my son. He is five years old and he is still cracking up hysterically to Patty Cakes.

New parents may not know what to do to entertain an infant. Remember everything you do with them is completely new. They are sponges at this age. Every word, sound, smell, taste, song, and facial expression is new to them. They are ready for learning and growing. Doing these rhymes reinforces that.

Lesson 10
Children Sleep in Their Own Crib/Bassinette - ONLY

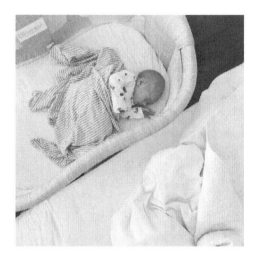

Children Sleep in Their Own Crib/Bassinette…no sleeping with mom and dad.

In my experience, I know this was a difficult challenge for my wife in the first two weeks. There are certain risks involved with the child being in the bed with the parents at a young age such as SIDS (Sudden Infant Death Syndrome). This made it easier for my wife to accept him not sleeping in the bed with us. In *Twelve Hours in Twelve Weeks,* it said we needed to create habits for healthy sleeping. The book suggested the baby should never sleep in the bed with the parents because it creates a co-dependency on the parents for comfort and the baby does not learn to self soothe.

Our solution: we moved the bassinet next to our bed. In the first few weeks, the bassinet was right next to our bed. Within a few weeks, we were able to transition him into his bedroom and eventually into his crib. He has slept in our bed very few times, such as when he has been sick or when he wet his bed in the middle of the night during potty training. He has never slept in our bed two nights in a row. Even when we travel we have a blow-up bed for him.

Lesson 11
Find Their Tickle Spots

Find Their Tickle Spots - Tickle Monster.

"Tickle me daddy. Tickle me!!" These are words that make me smile, laugh and overwhelm me with a sense of fulfillment.

I often tell my son his laugh is one of my favorite sounds in the world. To hear your child happy through uncontrollable laughter is amazing. At the time of writing this part, he is nearly six years old and just recently we did some Tickle Monster. He said, "Tickle me daddy. Tickle me!!" It brought me back to when he was just over a year old and his vocabulary was very limited. He knew maybe twenty words, but "tickle me" were some of his first words.

Find your child's tickle spots and explore them. Nothing is better than hearing them laugh!

Lesson 12
Speak to Them as if They Understand You NOW

Speak to them as if They Understand You Now – airplane ride at 6 months (Be aware of your surroundings)

This goes along with the previous lesson. As parents, we do not know when they are able to understand; all we can do is feed them the information. When my son was approximately six months old we often traveled on airplanes. We often traveled on early morning flights when people are typically tired. As he and I were walking down the aisle of the plane, I was telling him to be aware of his surroundings. I pointed out that we are in a small space, that many people are going to be uncomfortable in this space, and we would only be on the plane for short period of time. I told him to be respectful and behave.

As I got comfortable and got him buckled into his seat, a woman across the aisle expressed that he was just a baby and didn't understand what I was saying. I decided to educate her.

I explained to her that I have to teach him the lessons now, through actions and words. If I choose to start teaching the lessons when I feel he's able to receive them, then it may be too late. I told her that I always give him lessons, not knowing when he's going to be able to receive them. If he has heard them time and time again, when it is time for him to actually receive it, he will have not only heard it once; it will be a way of life for him. My goal is to have him evaluate situations, understand his surroundings, and respect those around him. If I were to start implementing those lessons when I felt he was ready to receive them, it could be too late.

I mention things that are important, therefore they become important to him. Teaching a child life lessons starts the day they are born; it starts through the actions of the parents and is reinforced with the explanation of the actions. When your actions are reinforced with the explanation, there's a greater understanding by the child. A small light bulb may go off and the child will think: this is why mom and/or dad do what they do. This creates a subconscious expectation of the child to behave in the same manner. Why? Because it is the only thing they have ever been taught through actions and words.

I continued to have conversations throughout the flight with my son. I did not get any more feedback from the lady on the other side of the aisle. He was also very well behaved.

Lesson 13
Never Say NO!

Never Say NO – it will be the first word they learn if you use it.

Many times, the first word or one of the first words children are comfortable saying is "No". This is because it is the word they hear most often. Encourage your children by creating scenarios that challenge their critical thinking skills.

Say yes to everything. The example I am going to give is for any child two years of age and older. I just did an interview with Dr. Keith Jowers. He mentioned on his website that I "Say Yes to Everything". He posed this question to me. "Too often parents are saying yes and there aren't enough no's being told to children. Do you agree with this?"
He then rephrased the question: "Do you believe that kids today need to be told NO more often? "

My response was that I say yes to everything that my child asks for. I do not say no. I give him options and allow him to choose based on those options. By giving him options, that allows him to say yes while at the same time saying no to the other option. This takes some critical thinking on my part, but it also allows for him to develop his critical thinking.

I gave Dr. Jowers this example: My son and I were at Target the other day and he asked for a toy. I said, "Yes, you can have the toy." But I gave him two options.

Option 1: YES! You can put it on your Christmas list for Santa Claus (as it was mid-October).

Option 2: YES! You can remind daddy in two weeks and we can pick it up then.

Did I say no? No. I gave him options. All children want a lot of toys; they are always going to ask. Why should I continually tell him no? In life, if we hear 'No' enough times we stop asking for things. When we stop asking for things we stop getting the results we desire. I do not want to impede his growth and thirst for knowledge by continually shutting him down. So instead, I choose to give him choices.

How does the scenario play out? If that particular toy is important enough for him he will put it on his Christmas list. We will continually revise the Christmas list until it's time for it to be delivered to Santa. If it makes it to the final list for Santa Claus, he will get that toy.

If he chooses the other option, which is to come back in two weeks, he has to remind me of that specific toy. If he really wants it, he will remember. If he reminds me, which tells me it is important enough to him, then I will get the toy. This avoids impulse buys and it also lets him know that he can have anything he wants, if he is willing to sacrifice time.

I never told him no. He has discovered that he needs to write it down on his Christmas list or remember what is important to him. Taking those actions then rewards him. He is not rewarded for just asking.

Ninety percent of the time he doesn't remember. Why? Because he's five years old and he asks for everything. He does not really want those things he just desires them in the moment. However, those things that are extremely important, the other ten percent, he is rewarded with. My wife and I make sure he gets those things because they are important and he reminds us. This strategy nullifies ninety percent of the No's.

It can be tiresome on a parent to continually say no. It's challenging for a child to critically think every time they ask for something. Get them thinking.

Lesson 14
Give Directions

Give Directions.

Tell children what you want them to do, not what you don't want them to do. Children have a hard time processing all of the words.

Examples:

"Don't spill your milk." Believe it or not, children hear, "Spill your milk."

"Don't run in the house." Children hear, "run in the house."

How do you change the terminology? Tell them what you actually want them to do.

"Be careful and aware. You have milk next to you and it could spill, if you are not careful."
"I would prefer that you walk in the house. Running is an outside activity."

Lesson 15
Play Music

Play Music for your kids.

Music brings life to the soul. Children remember things through music. That is why there are so many kids' songs and nursery rhymes. Music and singing are learning connectors. Children will naturally move when they hear certain songs. Music brings joy, laughter, motion, and emotion. Play uplifting child friendly music. In addition, play music that you enjoy so your child witnesses how you enjoy music too.

If you think back to your own childhood or adolescence, some of your more profound memories may include music. For our family and me the holidays come to mind. Christmas carols are a big part of holiday tradition. There is typically music playing in the background when we are celebrating any gathering.

In our home, we decided to get a Karaoke machine. Some of the earliest videos we have are of him singing and rocking out to Wheels on the Bus. These are opportunities to connect and grow as a family and it's as simple as putting your favorite music on in the background and letting your children see the joy it brings to you.

Just recently I caught my five year old singing every commercial that came on the television. I realized that there are songs from commercials that still linger in my mind 30+ years later. Music connects us in so many ways; make sure to use it as a tool to connect your family.

Lesson 16
Just Dance

Just Dance.

If you're playing music and you feel the need to, dance to it. Dance is another form of artistic expression like music… feel it. It is joyous, emotional and expressive. As early as my son was able to support his own head we put music on and swirled him around the house. Move and enjoy dancing to the music. Some of the biggest belly laughs I've ever gotten from my son as a baby were when we just danced around the room.

As children get older they will dance because you made it fun and encouraged it. Dance, even if it's uncomfortable for you. This is not about you, but the development of your child (I say this because I'm not a dancer normally, but I encourage you to dance with your child as I have done).

Go to YouTube and type in "Just Dance". Videos come up of the game "Just Dance". Your kids will love mimicking them and you do not even need to buy the game.

Lesson 17
Encourage Physical Activity

Encourage Physical Activity.

Children have lots of energy. Utilize that energy for good. I recently read a statistic that the average three-year-old takes seventy-five more steps per hour than the average adult.

Encourage even more movement than that. This can be done throughout their life. Children will mimic what you do. Go out and get exercise and bring them with you. All kids love the park, slides, and everything that a park has to offer. Encourage them to run, play, and take risks. They'll learn to understand their limits; just be there to catch them if they happen to fall.

Play games like tag and hide and go seek. These games encourage laughter, fun, and creativity. They also yield the best result of all, an exhausted child that sleeps really well.

When my son turned five, we were at the park and he saw an older child climbing a tree. He wanted to climb the tree too. I said go ahead. While being in close proximity, I witnessed him climb the tree over six feet high and the look of accomplishment on his face was awesome!

However, a couple minutes later he slipped and he was caught in the tree branches hanging on for his life. He was still six feet up in the air, hanging upside down, with his legs caught between branches. I was only fifteen feet from him and was able to go and help him get out. He had an accident without major repercussions. It was a learning experience for him. Now he will be more careful because he understands he can fall.

Lesson 18
Build Puzzles

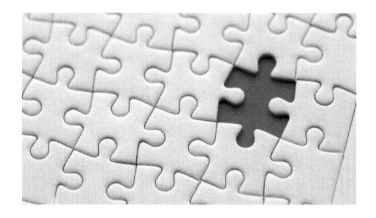

Building puzzles and doing projects.

Puzzles help children think differently. Seeing objects in different ways teaches them patience and that it takes time to complete a task. I also suggest puzzles that are beyond a child's age range (whatever it says on the box). It is our job as parents to challenge our children and to push them beyond societal boundaries.

My wife bought a 1000-piece puzzle for Father's Day for him and me to do together. It took three weeks to complete. He learned patience and organization. He also gained the experience of completing a long task. He did not do much, but he was present for the majority of the puzzle. He now demonstrates patience in doing his work at school. I believe it is because we have done large puzzles that take a tremendous amount of time and patience.

Most children want to do the different things that they see on television, whether it is building Legos or creating a hand puppet out of the paper bag. It is essential that we encourage these projects. As parents, we must also allow our children to do the majority of the work with some assistance if they have never done it before.

Example: We had to make snack bags for soccer practice one day for the entire team. Although my wife and I gathered the supplies, we allowed our son to pick the treats that he wanted his team to have. He put the variety of snacks (four different small snacks) in all twelve bags along with stickers for each bag (his idea). This was a small project. Encourage your children to do some of the work with all family projects.

Because he was a large part of the project, he wanted to be the one handing the bags out to his friends. He was proud that he made them. It taught him a sense of accomplishment.

After the soccer game, he said he wanted to make a puppet out of one of the brown bags. I asked him what supplies we would need. He said a brown paper bag, pink paper, black and blue paper, scissors, glue, and a pencil. I had no clue what he wanted to make or how he wanted to make it, I just started asking questions.

"What kind of puppet?" He said, "I think we should make a dog, dad."

"What does it look like?" He said, "It is going to have big ears dad. It is going to have blue eyes and put the nose right here, dad. It's going to have a big pink tongue right here dad."

I did not just go and get the supplies; I asked him what supplies he needed. I drew the eyes, the ears, and the tongue. He colored, cut, and glued them. We had our pet puppet bag in no time. It was a half hour project and a full day of fun.

He was able to make the decisions and do most of the work. He expressed himself artistically and he had a blast doing it.

Lesson 19
Building Blocks

Building Blocks and Destroying Them.

My son, as far back as I can remember, would stack blocks. You know the wooden ones with the letters, numbers, and different colors with animals on them. These are great learning tools. We would sit for hours stacking them. I would describe the animals on them and make the sounds that the animals make. I would point out the different letters and numbers. Then we would stack them. I would do one and he would do one. He would knock them over and we would laugh. He would want me to rebuild them. Then we learned to build them so high the tower would be taller than him. The challenge was to see how tall we could make it without it falling.

I just did it to make him laugh and learn. The best part was when we would go out to breakfast somewhere and he would take the individual coffee creamers and stack them seven or eight high on the table.

He enjoyed stacking everything. One of my favorite days was at about eighteen months old. He moved the step stool to the kitchen counter where my wife's Keurig coffee machine is. Next, he pulled out the drawer where all of her K-cups were. Then he stacked them about nine high on the kitchen counter.

Was I scared he might fall? Yes! Did I respond that way? NO!! I literally grabbed my phone and snapped a photo; I was excited he saw something he wanted to do and went after it.

This is foundational learning at its best and it starts with fundamentals.

My son stacking K-Cups at 18 months of age.

Lesson 20
Paint, Color, Draw

Paint, Color, Draw.

You do not have to be an artist to encourage your child to be creative. They're naturally very creative. Get them coloring books. I encourage you to color with them. They have never seen it done before; they are new to this world. They will learn by watching and mimicking you. How else will they learn?

At around two years old my son asked me to draw Mickey Mouse for him. I did it on large paper and drawing became a project on a weekly basis. We went on to draw many pictures of his favorite Disney characters. Buzz Lightyear, Lightning McQueen, Jake and the Neverland Pirates, and many more. He loved putting them up around his playroom. More importantly, he saw the process of drawing it, erasing it, and fixing it. Once it was drawn it then had to be colored. I like to think watching the process has helped him with his patience when doing his work at school. He understands that things do not necessarily happen quickly. It takes focused energy over time and lots of patience.

We continue to paint wooden airplanes, cars, trains, etc. He is getting better and better at it and we can spend an entire afternoon on a weekend, talking, laughing, painting and building toys. This is time to bond. That may not happen if we do not slow down and create.

Lesson 21
Throw the Ball

Throw the Ball or Have Some Tea.

Just engage with your child's natural tendencies. Boys are naturally more physical than girls, so I would encourage you to go throw rocks into a pond, skip stones, throw a baseball, or run in the park. In my experience being around young girls, they want to playhouse, dress-up dolls, set up the table and have conversation while drinking tea. These things reinforce and cultivate their very natural instincts and abilities. Although a dad may not want to sit and have a cup of tea, it's allowing your daughter to have quality time with you. Moms who may be reading this: if your son wants you to throw a baseball, he is telling you that you are important enough to him that he wants to share his physical abilities with you. Dad does not have to be good at having tea; your daughter will show you how. Moms do not have to throw strikes at 100mph; they just need to get the ball back to their sons. Our children are not judging us; they just want to share time with us.

Engage, indulge, and spend time with your children. That is all they want.

Lesson 22
Build Forts with the Sofa

Build forts and castles with the sofa.

Building forts and castles in the living room as a child, I used to grab all the pillows off of the couch and grab sheets. I even went as far as to get a box fan to blow the sheets higher. I did not teach my son to build forts. He just started moving pillows one day. He would say, "Daddy look at the tunnel I built. Look at my fort on the couch. Daddy can we build it bigger? Can we build it better? How?" We gathered the dining room chairs, more sheets and more pillows from other rooms. This is how the fort building began in our house.

Encourage their creativity. Let them build forts, as one day they maybe building real homes.

Building forts gives them a sense of pride and accomplishment. I would much rather pick up a messy living room after a day of creativity than have a perfectly clean living room and child mindlessly staring into a television.

Building forts in the living room turned into "Movie Night" (discussed a little further in the book). He wanted to "camp out" in the living room in his fort/tents. Because we were camping we would put on a movie. Camping isn't always part of Movie Night, but Movie Night has been a family staple on Friday nights.

Lesson 23
Reward the Behavior You Desire

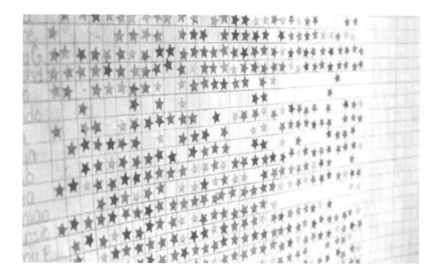

Reward the Behavior you Desire.

I do not know how this ended up to so far down the list, but it is a very simple concept. As parents, we can get caught up in teaching our children how to behave. We often criticize or remind them of what not to do. But we also need to reward them for the behavior that we desire. I often remind my son why he gets the things he desires. I'll ask the question, "Why do you get all of these things?"His response, "because I'm a good boy." My goal is to continually remind him of the reason he gets these things is because he earned them. He is also very aware if he is not a good boy, he may not get some other things he desires. His desires are toys, desserts, going to the park, and doing projects. If he is not being well behaved and doing what is expected of him, some of those things start to get taken away. He is reminded that if he is not well behaved, he will not be rewarded for poor behavior.

A great example of this is how we potty trained our son. Most kids like chocolate. We told him that if he were to go potty or pee pee in the toilet, he would get one M&M. He did this for several weeks and every time he went potty in the toilet he would get an M&M reward for the behavior we desired (him not peeing in his underwear or anywhere else except the toilet). It took three weeks for us to discover that one M&M was not enough for him to go poop. We decided to increase the reward for every time he went poop. For every time he pooped in the toilet, he would receive two M&Ms. The day we made that deal was a good one. He has never worn a diaper since.

Do not assume that your children know how you want them to behave. The only way they know is if you reward them for the behavior you desire. They will duplicate the behavior because they enjoyed the reward. Great rewards are: candy, stickers, stamps, and small toys. Rewards do not have to be big, they can be anything. Children like the recognition!

Lesson 24
Squeeze Lemons

Squeeze lemons (taste them too).

Children are naturally curious about a lot of things. They are not concerned with making or not making a mess. When I say squeeze lemons, it means to allow them to explore their natural curiosity. If it cannot harm them, let them explore. I have witnessed many parents say, "That will make a mess!" Let them make a mess today, so they do not make a mess of their lives later.

We enjoyed when our son started exploring new foods and tastes. One day when we were in a restaurant, the water server came with a lemon. My wife and I wanted him to taste it, just to get the facial expression. What he wanted to do was feel the lemon, squeeze it, and then eventually taste it.

As human beings, how we do anything is how we do everything. With every new adventure children want to experience it with all their senses. The only experience we wanted for him was to taste it. It was all new to him, he wanted to feel it, smell it, taste it, look at it, and even hear it hit the floor after it flew out of his hand. Children want to use all of their senses when something new is presented to them. Allow them that process.

Lesson 25
Let Them Take Risks

Let Them Take Risks. Let them be fearless.

Children understand their limits more then we give them credit for. We must allow them to take certain risks. A child will never learn to walk if the child does not fall. Children will never learn how to talk if they do not first mispronounce certain words. It is all a learning process. It is our job as parents to make sure we allow them to take certain calculated risks.

I mentioned earlier that my son climbed a tree for the first time. Why did he do it? He witnessed another kid around the same age doing it. It looked like fun and he knew he was capable. He was prepared because he has played on the playground and climbed things his entire childhood. He never even thought to climb a tree until he saw another child of similar capability doing it. He asked my permission to try it. I said yes without hesitation. Internally I was scared for him, but I knew allowing him to take those risks would progress his learning. As parents, we want them to be fearless and take those chances. If we are not conscious of these moments, we have a tendency to tell them everything that can go wrong.

When we are ready as parents, we then want them to try. It's our job as parents to encourage them while their minds are limitless.

If we only encourage them when we feel they are ready, then all they may remember are the consequences you instilled in them. They are full of fear and do not want to attempt those things. Do not to let your fears hinder your child's growth.

I witnessed this at the park recently. A ten-year-old child was learning to ride a bike for the first time. His parents were visibly frustrated that he had fear riding a bike. Why did they wait until ten? Could it have been their fears? Could it be their lack of belief in his abilities? It was probably a combination of several factors. At this point he was FULL OF FEAR surrounding his ability to ride a bike. He may have been told at five that he could not do it. He might have been told he would fall and get hurt or that he is clumsy. I am just making assumptions with those statements. Regardless of what may have been said, fear is taught.

My son is five as I write this book. I have referenced numerous events that have happened recently. This past weekend, he fell out of a tree onto the sidewalk. Running full speed after his soccer ball, he fell and scraped his hip and elbow. He banged his head against the glass dining room table because he did not realize how close he was to it as he went after our cat underneath the table. Standing near the table, he bent down and hit his forehead really hard on the glass. All of these experiences are learning opportunities. The consequences at this age are: a scrape, a bruise, or a bump on the forehead. Without these minor setbacks there may or may not be much learning. My mother always said mistakes are good as long as you learn from them.

Lesson 26
Go Hiking

Go Hiking or for Walks.

One of my favorite things I do with my son is going for walks, in what we call "The Spooky Forest." It is a wooded area on a trail we have near our home. You do not need a "Spooky Forest" to enjoy a walk with your child. Fresh air and conversation coupled with some exploration can build a bond that will last a lifetime. We have some of the best talks on our walks. We bond through exploration. I encourage him to use all of his senses while we are exploring. We listen for birds chirping, we touch the bark of trees, we smell the fresh air.

We only truly know what we experience in life. Later, when we read about these things in books, he has a greater understanding because of those experiences.

Lesson 27
Go to the Park and Play

Go to the Park and Play.

Kids learn so many social and physical skills by being at a park. They learn to engage and play with other kids they may or may not know. They experience climbing, taking risks, laughing, playing, and even getting up after getting hurt. They continue to play because they are in an environment that encourages it. Go to the park as often as you can. It will encourage them to get out of their comfort zone. More importantly, it will encourage you as a parent to get out of your own comfort zone. Encourage them to go down the slides when they are two. Then encourage them to climb stairs, poles, monkey bars, and rock walls. Before you know it, they will no longer need your assistance. You will use these same skills as parents until they become adults.

Parks are a fundamental building block of growth, providing an environment that is fun and encourages doing things outside of their comfort zone. It allows them to develop skills such as engaging with others, and resolving conflicts. All of these things are building a foundation for a well-rounded child in a fun environment

Lesson 28
Feed the Ducks and Geese

Feed the Ducks and Geese. Engage with dogs and cats.

Children need to respect, connect and explore with all living creatures by allowing them to understand the body language of other animals. Animals are not capable of speaking but they do give clear signs that say, "I'm about to attack. I'm scared. I'm hungry. I'm friendly."If a child understands the body language of a dog and or a cat by having a pet, they will also intuitively start to read body language signs of human beings and understand the dangers of other animals or even other adults. Children are very intuitive and rely more on senses than communication. This can be enhanced by putting animals into the mix. When we go feed the ducks I always tell my son to be aware of their body language when we have food. They are coming with confidence because they know they are about to be fed. However, they are also animals and we need to respect their space, their strength and what it is that they want, so do not tease them and give them the food at a distance.

It is the same thing with the ducks. They may fight with each other over the food that we are giving them, as they are in survival mode. Do not give them the opportunity to fight you for the food. I always point out the behavior of the animals.

When a child meets a dog for the first time, instruct the child to show the dog the backside of their hand. This creates a non-threatening environment for the dog to connect. It shows that the child respects the dog. Once the dog's body language says okay, then the child can pet it.

It is no different in human behavior. Approach people in a non-threatening way and you will get the same reciprocation.

If a child can understand animal behavior, the child will inherently bring that same subconscious understanding into their human behavior. The way your child treats animals will probably be the same way they treat their human interactions.

Having said that...It is very important that you teach your child to respect animals at a high-level.

Lesson 29
Share Your Passions

Share Your Passions and Connect.

One thing I am extremely passionate about is football. I find it interesting that not too long ago my wife expressed her displeasure that our son has not yet learned to catch a football. As a father, I have chosen not to have expectations that my son will enjoy all the same things that I do.

I believe we can naturally connect through the sport without it being forced. He is at an age where he finally watches games with me, but I do not expect that of him. We talk about the score and if he has questions, I answer them. Overall, he is not highly interested. However, he does know all of the football teams.

We have a friendly football pool with other family members and he gets to pick all of the games. We count how many wins and losses we have every week. We read graphs of who is winning and losing. He understands how much a touchdown is scored and how much they are worth. He understands a field goal is different than an extra point and is worth three points versus one. He understands offense and defense. He is excited when I tell him our team is playing and whether or not they won or lost.

More than watching the game, I enjoy the common interest of competition. He is a competitor and he likes to win. It is exciting to watch it unfold in his personality development. I have never told him that he needs to win, because nobody ever told me that I needed to win. He wants to win; it's natural.

What I chose to focus on is the *effort* when playing anything, not the result. As a dad, it is exciting to see some of the same traits in my son. Seeing these traits comes from spending an immense amount of time with him. I appreciate them for what they are, not what I am telling him he needs to do.

Lesson 30
Be Your Childs Hero

Be Your Childs Hero.

When I started creating the outline for this book and I wrote, "Be Your Kids Hero," the story I'm about to tell had not yet happened. We were getting ready for bath-time one evening and he noticed that my computer was up and running a Word document. It was this book. He asked me what it was and I said, "It's a book that I'm writing about you." He was at the stage of learning to write his own words and sound them out. He asked if he could write some words. I very quickly made sure my work was saved and said, "Please. Go ahead. What word do you want to spell?" He said, "Zero." We proceeded to sound out the word and he typed it. He then asked how to spell the word hero. I mentioned that it rhymed with the word zero, which meant that it is spelled similarly. I asked him what letter it began with. He then proceeded to spell the word and type it in on his own.

When he was done, he asked if he had done it correctly. I checked it and he had. I then looked at him and asked him who his hero was. My expectation was he would say Superman, Batman, Hulk, Captain America or any of the other super heroes that he was familiar with.

To my pleasant surprise, without hesitation, he said, "Daddy, you are."For a parent who puts as much energy and effort into their child as I do, no greater words could have been spoken.

All of these things I'm discussing in this book are about spending time and making a conscious effort to insure the time you spend is quality time and well thought out. Even if it is not well thought out, all our children want is our time; all they want is us. They love their parents unconditionally, good or bad because we are what they know. We are where they came from. If you do not believe me here is a quick test you can run mentally through your head. I do not suggest actually doing it.

Some parents believe that giving their children all the material things in the world is what they want. Here is the test.

Ask your child if they want to go to Toys "R" Us.
(They recently went out of business ☹ so choose your favorite toy store instead)

The answer will be yes.

Go to your toy store of choice and bring them to their favorite section of that store. Tell your child that they can have everything in this store that they want. Then attempt to leave them there. After all, they have everything that they "want". Let them know that they will never see you again because they have everything that they "want". Start walking away and see if your child <u>wants</u> all those toys or if they <u>want</u>

you and your time (you do not have to actually do this exercise). You know what the answer is. They will take you over all of that stuff, 24 hours a day, 7 days a week.

If you know this to be true in your heart, start giving more of yourself today. Just about every lesson in this book is about giving more of yourself.
The best way to be your child's hero is to give them you, your time, and your attention.

Cristian was typing this below during the writing of this book.

Play zero do   hero

Lesson 31
Ask them to Repeat Words
They Are Learning to Speak

Ask them to Repeat Words They Are Learning to Speak. Can you say...?

We are teaching our children how to speak when we introduce new words to them. Very simply say to them, "Can you say car?" They will repeat the word. This must be a continual thing throughout every day when they get to the age when they are speaking. It takes time, energy, effort, and focus. When your child is speaking with clarity and pronouncing words that are not expected of them, it is because they have practiced. It is because you have done your job and asked them to repeat the words they are learning. If they do not pronounce it correctly, praise them for the attempt. If they are just learning to speak, chances are they will not get it right, but if you praise their effort they will eventually get it. As they get older, you can make corrections when it is age appropriate. Make it fun. When they say the word wrong do not correct them. Encourage them for saying it the way that they said it and laugh hysterically if it is not perfect. They will want to say it again and again and again. They made you happy!! They made you laugh. They will learn to say it correctly through hearing it multiple times, but if they are reprimanded or constantly corrected it is no longer fun.

Allow them to learn at their pace. They will rarely say the word correctly the first time. If it is the first time they are doing something, it should not be expected for them to do it right. What should be expected is that they continually attempt to say the word because it is fun to say the word. It makes mom and/or dad laugh. That is fun.

Lesson 32
Celebrate All Successes

Celebrate All Successes….Big and Small. Encourage them.

The previous lesson leads right into celebrating all successes. Attempting to walk for the first time is a success. When our baby stood for the first time under his own strength we celebrated it. We made a big deal out of it. When our son took his first step, it was celebrated. When he first fell, we laughed and picked him up and congratulated him for the success he had, we did not focus on the fall. We celebrated it all.

When a child says the word burger and it sounds like booger we should celebrate it, not correct them. Celebrate for the attempt to say it correctly just as you celebrate for the attempt to walk.

Try to remember to focus on all of the successes. When a child colors for the first time and they color outside of the lines or they color the sun purple, encourage them for being different. Let them know it looks amazing. Let them know coloring is a fun experience and mom and dad are going to support whatever it is that they do.

With time and repetition the sun will become yellow. With time and repetition they will no longer color outside of the lines. With time and practice they will no longer be coloring in a circular motion, but all shading in the same direction and consistency.

With practice, they will come to draw their own sun, in their own pictures. Who knows, they may be an illustrator of coloring books one day, but only if it has been a fun experience. So, always encourage whatever they are doing even though it may not be perfect. All you are really doing is encouraging them to do something that will turn into amazing things.

Lesson 33
Watch the Olympic Games

Watch the Olympics Games.

The lessons learned through watching the Olympics have been tremendous. Throughout my life my family has gathered together to watch the Summer Olympics and celebrate our country through sport. My wife's experience of The Olympics was different; it was not a focal point of the home. When I told her it was very important to me that we watch the Olympics together, she originally did not see the fascination. She soon found the value in our son watching the Olympics with us, as a family. Each evening from 8:00pm until he went to bed around 9:00pm we would watch. I would record the Games and we would watch in the early evenings too.

In school, they were talking about the different countries and he started learning about the flags. He started learning about some of our Olympic heroes, such as Michael Phelps. When the Olympics started and the opening ceremonies had Michael Phelps bringing the American flag into the stadium, my son got very excited. He became very patriotic and wanted to cheer on his country, the United States.

He also started learning about competition, about winning, and sportsmanship.

He was asking about all of the different flags of the different countries. He wanted to look at a map and see where these countries were. He wanted to understand the difference between first, second, and third place. He wanted to understand what the gold, silver, and bronze medals represented. He learned the excitement of winning and all of us winning as a country.

He also experienced the disappointment of losing and not getting medals. We talked about the hard work that these athletes put in for years and years and years to get to this level.

At the end of the Olympics, he wanted to write a letter to some of the Olympians thanking them for representing our country. His favorite sports were volleyball, gymnastics and of course swimming as Michael Phelps did extremely well once again.

He learned nearly all of the flags of all the countries represented in the Olympics in the few weeks that we watched the Olympics. He learned about sportsmanship, excitement, disappointment, hard work and appreciation for other countries. He also learned about patriotism. The lessons from watching the Olympics, as a family, have been invaluable and in my opinion not as easily taught without sport, specifically the Olympic sports.

Lesson 34
Create Traditions

Create Traditions.

This can be anything from carving pumpkins at Halloween, to strawberry picking in the Spring to movie night every Friday. When I was growing up, some of my favorite memories were the holiday traditions. When I was really young we would watch the Wizard of Oz when it came on TV once a year. On other nights, my mother would make me a weekly treat to watch certain TV Shows. We'd have popcorn one week and other weeks we'd have ice cream sundaes or baked brownies or cookies. The point is, we did it consistently and we did it together. It was a gathering/tradition. I looked forward to it and I still remember it today.

One of the traditions in our home now is Movie Night every Friday. This has been going on for nearly a year. I mentioned it earlier in the Build Forts Lesson, that Movie Night began with my son wanting to camp in his fort in the living room on the weekends. We started watching movies while we camped.

Every Friday night we order out, we have an early dinner, and get ready for bed. We pick our movie of the week (usually by Wednesday) and by 7:00pm on Friday night we are on the sofa with our popcorn and treats watching our movie. The forts are optional but movie night is here to stay.

Recently we attended a Friday Night Movie night at my son's school in their parking lot. Many of the children were playing on the playground and amongst their friends. Before the movie my son was also playing. As the movie began, we set up our chairs in front of the big blown-up screen and my son got on my reclining chair and laid back on my chest, just like we were at home snuggling on the sofa.

I looked around and many of the kids were consumed with playing and being out late on a Friday night. I said to my son "It's ok if you want to go play with your friends." He looked back at me and said, "It's our movie night, I want to watch the movie with you."

That one sentence made all of the Disney movies I have sat through over the last year worth every moment. I will never forget my 5-year-old choosing our tradition over all the other FUN that was going on around us.

Lisa's Top 6
(Lessons 35-40)

After compiling the first 34 Lessons and outlining this book, I knew that I had missed some very obvious things that my wife and I have done over the first five years of our son's life.

I decided to ask her what she felt were some key things we do regularly that are impacting our son positively.

Her immediate response was, "We do not do anything special, we just do what we are supposed to do." I will admit I don't feel that everything I've shared up to this point is "special". It really is not special if you do it once or even twice. It only becomes special if you do it consistently.

Dads, I'll give a sports analogy. As a football fan, it does not impress me when a running back scores a touchdown. That is his job.

Creating a tradition, but not repeating it doesn't make it a tradition. Going on a hike with your child once does not create a bond. Going to the park once a year does not allow your child to take enough risks to learn from.

Just like that running back scoring a touchdown does not impress me, doing these things once, or seldom, does not make you a great dad.

But what if that running back scores 20+ touchdowns a season or 100+ over his career. Consistency makes that running back great.

You showing up consistently in these areas will make you a great father. You too can celebrate in the end zone of parenthood.

After my wife said we do not do anything special, I shared with her the first 10 lesson titles and I elaborated a little bit on each one. Her response was, "Wow, I did not realize how much energy and effort we have put into him."

It doesn't seem special because we are in the middle of it and we do it every day; however, we have applied a great deal of energy and focus into how we want to approach raising our son. She then came up with the next six lesson titles that I think are invaluable. I happened to overlook these and I'm sure many more.

I want to share them with you.

Lesson 35
Tell Them "I Love You"

Always tell your children how much you love them. They will never question that.

This seems so simple. That is probably why I left it off the list. My son probably hears this from my lips fifteen to twenty times a day. However, I not only tell him, I show him through my actions by applying the previous 34 Lessons. He not only hears it, but it is reinforced with our actions as parents. One would think that a parent would not have to tell their child, "I love you," but saying it leaves no doubt in their minds.

I have encountered too many people that say they never heard "I love you" come from their parents' mouths. Do not let that be your child. You may be one of those children. Break the cycle.

Lesson 36
Clean Up Time

Clean up time.

He puts his things where they belong. Everything has a place. Clean up after you play. Respect your possessions. It's easier for him to know where his toys are.

I will preface this particular lesson with this: I am not the most organized individual on the planet. This lesson is attributed to my wife. I love that our son does this. My wife takes great pride in a clean home.

Our son knows how to pick up after himself. He normally cleans up after playing but if he doesn't, there is always a time of the day where we pick up his toys together. My wife has put a lot of energy and effort into teaching him to respect his toys and to put them where they belong. He has become very detailed as to where everything goes. All of his toys are in great shape, as if they were just taken out of the package; and he knows where everything is. If anything is missing, and I do mean anything (I'm talking one Lego piece here), he questions it and wants to know where it is. He respects his toys not only by the way he plays with them, but also by putting them back where they belong each and every day.

I know some of you are thinking, *but aren't toys supposed to be played with and broken? Aren't kids supposed to be kids and play recklessly?* I remember having a battle with myself, wanting to tell my wife, just let him be a kid. My wife ultimately won, and I have to say that I believe it has instilled a level of appreciation and respect in him that will last him a lifetime.

How has this translated into the real world? When we visited his elementary school as a family, going into kindergarten, there was a tour of the library. There were several other families present. While other kids were taking books off of the shelves and throwing them on the floor, our son was going around picking up those same books off the floor and putting them back on shelves. That was a proud parenting moment.

To watch fifteen other children, disrespect a space, and to watch my child not only respect the space but clean up after the other children, that let me know what my wife and I have been doing over all these years is working. That brought an immense amount of joy to both me and my wife. He chose, amongst his peers, to respect and do the right thing. It's because we've taken the time, and given the energy and effort at home to teach and instill those lessons of respect.

Lesson 37
Create a Routine

Create a routine - Bed time, meal time, reading time.

This goes back to creating your schedule for your child, regardless of how chaotic your life is and I know your life is chaotic; you are a parent. We must create a level of consistency in our child's life regardless of the chaos. You maybe thinking *what would you know about chaos*? It seems as though your family has it *together*.

One of the many challenges we faced as a couple was being in a long-distance relationship for many years. My wife lived in Georgia while I lived in Florida. Our careers had us separated. We would travel back and forth on a weekly basis to visit each other. In the first year of our son's life, before I made a career change, he was on over forty flights. He was sleeping in different homes, in different states. He was visiting with different people. Although it was very chaotic, from the outside looking in, his routine never changed. He had a schedule. He woke up every day at the same time. He got fed to the minute at the same time. He played, napped and got changed at the same time. That only happened because a routine was created. Why? Because even his bowel movements become regular. He took his second nap at the same time every day. He was fed at the same times. He went to bed every night at the same time. Did we book flights around his schedule? Yes. Did we make sure bottles were prepared ahead of time to make sure he got fed at those times? Yes. Although our lives, our schedules, our travel, and where we stayed were very inconsistent, he knew his necessities were taken care of based on his routine. He knew he would be changed. He knew he would be fed consistently. He knew he would be in a place of comfort so that he could nap. He knew we would play with him. He knew he would have this consistency every day because that is how we showed up as parents. That takes time, energy, effort, and planning; but it's so worth it.

Example of his Schedule: Year 1

6:00 – Wake up – Immediate change
6:10 – Make bottle (together) and feeding
6:30 – 9:00 – Play, sing, entertain
9:00 – Change/Nap time
10:00 –Wake up Bottle
1:00 – Change/ Nap time
2:00 – Bottle, play, sing, learn, entertain.
6:00 – Bottle/Night Routine

Lesson 38
Daddy Talk Time

Daddy talk time.

Lisa added daddy talk time in here. This is something I started doing when he was about 4 years old. It is my bonding time with my son.

Our evening routine (there is that *routine* word again) is like this:

6:00 – 7:00 – Cook and have dinner
7:30 – 8:00 – Get ready for bed (vitamin, bath, brush teeth)
8:00 – In mom and dad's bed reading books (30-45 min)
8:30/8:45 – In bed – Prayers and Daddy talk time.

During the last 15-30 minutes of the day we do what I call daddy talk time. Daddy talk time consists of me asking him how his day was and what he learned during the day. I ask him at that point if he has any questions for me or if he wants to share anything with me. We typically do some type of learning during that time. I often utilize YouTube videos to answer his questions.

Example: He wanted to see how pumpkins grew during Halloween. We watched a pumpkin patch grow on an elapsed time video on YouTube (on the phone). It satisfied his craving, he learned, and it was a bonding experience.

I typically end daddy talk time by telling him five specific things he did during the day that made me proud.

That list can look something like this: (I reference the things he already shared with me during the conversations we had up to that point in the day)

> Today in school you stayed on color green (that means that he did not get in trouble for anything).
> That makes daddy proud.
>
> Today when mommy came home with groceries you helped her bring them in without us asking.
> That makes daddy proud.
>
> Today at soccer practice when one of your friends tripped and fell, you went over and lent a hand to pick them up.
> That makes daddy proud.
> When you lost the soccer game today you still went and shook everybody's hands and told them good game.
> That makes daddy proud.
>
> Tonight, when we said prayers, you thanked God for several things that daddy did not expect you to thank him for.
> That makes daddy proud.

I typically ask him one last question.

> Is there anything that you did today that daddy may have missed that you did because you know it makes daddy proud?

Sometimes his answer is no. Other times he will tell me something he did at school that I would not have otherwise known. Because I ask this question, he opens up and tells me another positive aspect of his day. I always reinforce and let him know those things do make me proud.

I have plenty to be proud of as his father. It makes him want to do more when I acknowledge it. Reward the behavior you desire, at least by acknowledging it.

Lesson 39
Communicate Change

Communicate Change.

Always let them know what is going on.

Kids often throw fits in public places. My belief is that it is because their expectations have not been met at some level. Children do not want to go to the mall to shop, but if they're told that they are going to go to the mall and they can prepare themselves mentally for that, it may be a different story.

Early on, my wife and I realized if our son knew exactly what was going on throughout his day there was less resistance. Therefore, we tend to tell him days in advance how our week is going to go so there are no unexpected surprises, whether good or bad.

For instance, if we are going to be in the car for nine hours, we let him know three days in advance. We make sure he understands that he is going to be in a confined space for a very long time. Kids have little or no concept of time, therefore we may reference by saying, "You could watch four movies in that time." We also start asking what we can do to make things more comfortable for him. Do you want an iPad? Which toys do you want to bring? What snacks would you like? Again, it goes into the planning, we have planned our week so we can share these things with him. He gets a say in what is going to make the trip comfortable for him. If those things are not making him comfortable during the trip, we reinforce those are the things he chose. We are not surprised if he becomes uncomfortable but because we have set the expectations we get very little push back. However, it is nothing near what we have heard other parents have experienced. Why? Because we were able to set the expectation in advance and he is not surprised.

Tell your children everything so that you can have more pleasant experiences. If you are prepared, they are prepared mentally. When you allow them to have a say in the preparation, it becomes a much more enjoyable experience.

This goes for all things, like starting school for the first time. Prepare them for the week and make it exciting. If you are excited, they will be excited. When he entered Kindergarten, from a Pre-K school we told him he was going to a big boy school and we said it with excitement. He was excited and still is months later.

The first time they have a baby sitter, be sure to introduce them to that person in advance. Don't just drop a stranger on your child. Let them know at some point this person may be watching them. When that time comes there are no surprises and possibly no push back.

If they are going to go to Disney World let them know it is going to be a very long and exciting day, but after the park they will be sleeping in a hotel, rather than at home. In their young minds, they may have an expectation that they are coming back home to their bed, but they do not know unless you tell them.

The more you tell them, the less they are surprised. The less surprised, the more enjoyable the experience is for everybody. It's all about communication with children. Everything I have talked about in this book has been about communicating and spending time at a high-level. The more you engage with your children the more fruit you will see from your labor.

The previous examples are of travel, but this works on a daily basis also. Let them know the day prior if there is something different happening in their routine.

Example: Daddy has to get to the office early tomorrow. He wants you to get your sleep. So when you get up, we will get ready for school and you will be having breakfast in the car tomorrow. You will be getting to school earlier than usual.

The normal routine is to get dressed and sit for breakfast while enjoying his favorite cartoon.

If the change is not communicated the night before and the routine he enjoys, watching his cartoon, is all of the sudden taken away from him, there will be tremendous resistance in the morning. All of that can be eliminated with simple communication the night before.

Lesson 40
Read Daily

Read Daily. Yes, Every Single Day.

Reading every day is something our family started doing when my son was six months old. It is something we do after bath time every single night.

There are very few occasions when we do not read. One exception to the rule is Movie Night. We are creating a tradition and are still doing something together. Other exceptions could be going to watch the fireworks on the Fourth of July, trick-or-treating for Halloween, going to a party at a friend's house and he just comes home exhausted, or watching the Olympics (a once every 4-year experience).

I would suggest to read every night; never use "no reading" as a punishment. Never use it as a penalty. Our child enjoys reading. He loves it. We learned this early on. It is connection time with mom and dad. You never want to say to your child, if you don't do this there are no books tonight. It's a learning tool. It is something that they want and need.

It's bonding time. They learn to read faster. They become comfortable with books. All of these things can be nothing but a positive experience for a child in their development long-term.

Leaders are readers. Lead by example as a parent to read to your child. Your child will pass that on generationally and become leaders themselves by having a thirst for stories, knowledge, and education.

After age five make sure your child reads at least 20 minutes a day. According to research, a child who reads only one minute a day outside of school will learn 8,000 words by the end of sixth grade where a student who reads 20 minutes outside of school will learn 18,000! That is huge! If reading isn't one of your child's top priorities, you may need to set up an incentive program.

I've created an incentive program over the summer. Going into the first grade they sent home a list of 100 words that he would have to read by the end of 1st grade. I gave him one star for every day he read. At the beginning of the summer he read 25 of those words, we went through the list until he mastered it. Then we would move to the next set of 25. Once all 100 were mastered he read through them all each day.

It was our goal each day to do the work and get a star. Those stars translated into $1.00 each at the end of the summer. Those 15-20 minutes a day that cost me a dollar were the best money and minutes of the day I spent all summer. He went into the first grade knowing all the words they expected him to know by the end of the year. He went from reader level D to a level A over the course of the year. This far exceeded any expectations.

His confidence is through the roof when it comes to reading and it created an atmosphere for him to desire reading all year long. It was the best $60 I have ever spent.

CLAIM YOUR FREE EXTRA RESOURCES

BLOG
VIDEOS
PODCAST
YOUTUBE
ETC.

Go To:

BeTheDadYouWishYouHad.com/Extra

Made in the USA
Columbia, SC
05 June 2019